LILIES

Lily

LILIES

BRIAN MATHEW

A ROMANTIC HISTORY WITH A GUIDE TO CULTIVATION

RUNNING PRESS
Philadelphia, Pennsylvania

Concept, design, and editorial direction Simon Jennings.
Produced, edited, and designed at Inklink,
Greenwich, London, England.

Text by Brian Mathew
Text edited by Geraldine Christy
Designed by Simon Jennings
Botanical illustrations by Julia Cobbold
Archive illustrations enhanced by Robin Harris

Published in The United States of America
by Running Press, Philadelphia, Pennsylvania

Text setting and computer make-up by Inklink, London.
Image generation by Blackheath Publishing Services, London.
Printed by Southsea International Press, Hong Kong.

Canadian representatives: General Publishing Co., Ltd.,
30 Lesmill Road, Don Mills, Ontario M3B 2T6.
International representatives: Worldwide Media Services, Inc.,
30, Montgomery Street, Jersey City, New Jersey 07302.

9 8 7 6 5 4 3 2 1
Digit on the right indicates the number of this printing.

Library of Congress Catalog Number 93-83528

ISBN 1-56138-304-X

This book may be ordered by mail from the publisher.
Please add $2.50 for postage and handling.
But try your bookstore first!
Running Press Book Publishers
125 South Twenty-Second Street
Philadelphia, Pennsylvania 19103

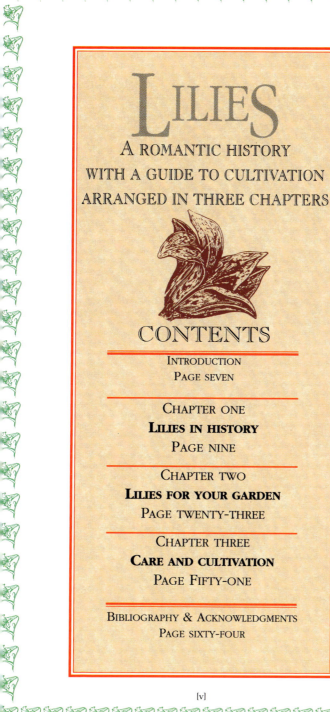

LILIES

A ROMANTIC HISTORY
WITH A GUIDE TO CULTIVATION
ARRANGED IN THREE CHAPTERS

CONTENTS

THE LILY

Have you seen but a bright lily grow,
before rude hands have touch'd it?
Have you marked but the fall o' the snow
Before the soil hath smutch'd it?
O so white! O so soft! O so sweet is she!
BEN JONSON (1573-1637)

INTRODUCTION

IT IS UNLIKELY THAT THE BIBLICAL "LILIES OF THE FIELD" referred to any particular plant, but rather to the colorful wild flowers of the Holy Land in general. The *Leirion* of the ancient Greeks also appears to have been a group name, possibly describing several bulbous plants. *Krinon basilikon*, however, known to Dioscorides, the Greek physician and herbalist (A.D. 40-90), can be precisely identified as the plant we know today as *Lilium candidum*.

Few true lilies were known to the early peoples of the Mediterranean, for the great majority of them originate from eastern Asia and North America, but those few figured prominently in artwork, herbal remedies, and as a source of perfume.

The medieval herbalists knew and utilized some additional lilies, but it was not until the eighteenth century, an era of great horticultural exploration, that many new species were discovered. The majority arrived in the gardens of Europe in the nineteenth century, but surprisingly the amazing *L. regale* and many other superb lilies from China were not known to western botanists and gardeners until the early twentieth century.

The hybridization of lilies was not really exploited until the present century when species from Europe, China, Japan, and the U.S.A. were brought together in controlled programs of breeding and selection to lay the foundations of the wonderful range of garden-worthy lilies available to us today. With such diversity of color and form which the many species provide, along with hardiness, ease of cultivation, and disease resistance, the modern plant breeder has almost unlimited possibilities.

The first section of this book explores the history of lilies, their artistic value, and their uses through the ages. The second section gives a description of the lily plant and a range of the most desirable species and cultivars, and the final section provides useful information on care and cultivation.

DEDICATED TO
OUR ENVIRONMENT
WHICH SUFFERS
IN SILENCE

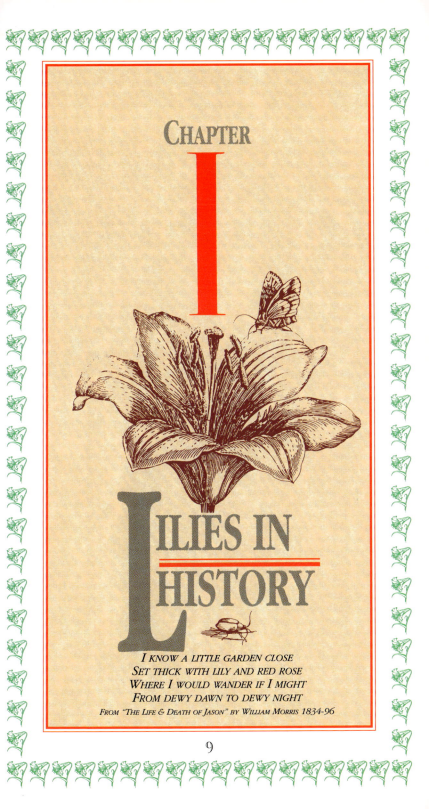

CHAPTER I

LILIES IN HISTORY

I KNOW A LITTLE GARDEN CLOSE
SET THICK WITH LILY AND RED ROSE
WHERE I WOULD WANDER IF I MIGHT
FROM DEWY DAWN TO DEWY NIGHT
FROM "THE LIFE & DEATH OF JASON" BY WILLIAM MORRIS 1834-96

Natural habitats of lilies

There are approximately one hundred species of *Lilium* known today, occurring solely in the northern hemisphere and primarily in the temperate regions. Their habitats are as varied as the lilies that grow in them, from sea level to an altitude of nearly 15,000ft (5000m),

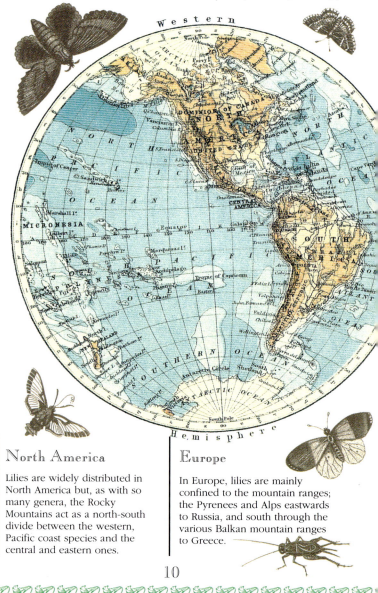

North America

Lilies are widely distributed in North America but, as with so many genera, the Rocky Mountains act as a north-south divide between the western, Pacific coast species and the central and eastern ones.

Europe

In Europe, lilies are mainly confined to the mountain ranges; the Pyrenees and Alps eastwards to Russia, and south through the various Balkan mountain ranges to Greece.

from marshes and cool damp woodlands to open sunny screes or rock crevices, on acid and alkaline soils and formations. Little wonder, then, that within this genus there is a lily to suit almost any garden.

Asia

In western Asia, notably Turkey and the Caucasus, there are few species. There is a vast area through Iran, Afghanistan, and Central Asia that is almost devoid of them. The Himalayan chain, too, is far from being richly endowed with lilies.

China and Japan are the treasure chests of the lily world. The former has provided us with a feast of garden-worthy species such as *L. regale*, *L. davidii*, *L. duchartrei*, *L. langkongense*, *L. sargentiae*, while Japan has added the astonishing *L. auratum*, as well as *L. dauricum*, *L. japonicum*, and *L. speciosum*. Not only are all these plants beautiful in their own right, but they have also given plant breeders the raw materials with which to create many new hybrids in colors and combinations not achieved in nature.

THE LILY COLLECTORS

THE LILIES WE KNOW TODAY have been introduced into our gardens over a long period of time, the earliest undoubtedly being the Madonna Lily, probably first "tamed" by the ancient Egyptians. Frescoes recently unearthed on the Greek island of Thera suggest that the scarlet *L. chalcedonicum* was cultivated there, possibly as early as 2000 B.C., and the ancient Greek writers certainly knew *L. candidum*. This subsequently became widely dispersed in the gardens of Europe for decorative and medicinal purposes, together with a few other European species, with the result that by the sixteenth century, *L. bulbiferum, L. chalcedonicum, L. martagon,* and the Madonna Lily were quite well known.

The discovery of the attractive and very distinct North American species raised considerable interest in Europe. Two of the first to be introduced were *L. canadense*, in the early seventeenth century, and *L. superbum* about 100 years later. The latter was so admired that the artist Georg Ehret was commissioned to produce a stunning painting of it in 1751, over ten years before Linnaeus christened the plant with the "superb" epithet it now bears.

The Asiatic species remained unknown until the nineteenth and early twentieth centuries, when many were discovered, named, and introduced. The Tiger Lily *(L. lancifolium)*, although cultivated for food by the Chinese over one thousand years ago, did not arrive in the West until 1804 when William Kerr sent some bulbs to Kew Gardens from Canton (now Guangzhou).

L. speciosum was introduced from Japan by Philipp von Siebold in the 1830s and this, in turn, was overshadowed by the "Queen of Lilies," *L. auratum*. This lily so captivated the public that there was an instant demand and, in 1864, only two years after its initial introduction, it was reported in the *Gardeners' Chronicle* that "a large quantity" of bulbs were auctioned at Covent Garden market, raising £1000 (about $1500). They had been sent "in common packing cases, round the Cape of Good Hope, in the hold of a sailing vessel, and must have been at least four or five months at sea . . . most of them were as plump and fresh as if they had been dug up and brought from some suburban nursery on the morning of the sale."

Carolus Linnaeus (1707-78)
Swedish botanist and founder of
BINOMIAL TAXONOMIC CLASSIFICATION
*(the classification of plants by
name).* Linnaeus *christened*
L. superbum *with the* "superb"
epithet it now bears.

Further Asiatic lilies arrived intermittently, including *L. longiflorum* which has become such an important cut flower, but the era of botanical exploration in China was to provide more treasures. Of the many collectors, Ernest Wilson figures most prominently in relation to lily discoveries. Wilson was employed as a plant collector by Veitch's nursery, England, and the Arnold Arboretum, U.S.A., and during the course of six expeditions gained an encyclopedic knowledge of lilies which he distilled into *The Lilies of Eastern Asia*, published in 1925. His major introductions were the magnificent *L. regale* and its close relative *L. sargentiae*, *L. davidii*, and *L. duchartrei*, all of which have proved to be excellent garden plants.

Although Wilson probably did more than anyone to increase our knowledge of wild Chinese lilies, there were many other collectors who explored China and whose names are commemorated in the plants they discovered, notably Paul Farges (the rare *L. fargesii*), Augustine Henry (*L. henryi*), Reginald Farrer (*L. farreri*, and introducer of *L. leucanthum centifolium*), George Forrest (*L. georgei*, and introducer of *L. taliense*), Frank Kingdon-Ward (*L. wardii*, and *L. mackliniae* named after his wife), and Joseph Rock, who made re-collections of several of the beautiful Chinese lily species.

Lily popularity reached a peak, and specialist nurseries, such as that of W. A. Constable of Tunbridge Wells, England, were devoted to the introduction and marketing of lilies. Around 70 species, as well as many hybrids and cultivars, were offered for sale in their 140-page catalog for 1938-39. Although the heyday of the lily explorers was more or less at an end, for the plant breeders life was just beginning.

13

LILIES TO COOK AND TO CURE

*"When you have only two pennies left in the world,
buy a loaf with one and a lily with the other."*

THIS CHINESE SAYING HAS MORE SENSE than at first appears.
After all, you could eat them both if necessary! In
spite of their great beauty, lilies have not always been
appreciated for solely aesthetic reasons, and no doubt
early man made good use of the fact that the bulbs were
comparatively large and edible.

It is likely that many of the species have been used for
food on a local scale in the distant past, but even in
recent times it is recorded that in Russia, for example,
L. martagon bulbs were dried and eaten with reindeer's
milk, and several of the North American species were a
source of food for various Native-American tribes. John
Veitch, who introduced *L. auratum* into cultivation in
1862, reported that the bulbs were "much sought after by
the Japanese for purposes of food. They are boiled and
eaten in much the same way as we do potatoes, and have
an agreeable flavor resembling that of a chestnut." Other
accounts are rather more specific about its culinary value:
"It can be powdered and used to make delicious
dumpling balls."

Although not brought into western gardens until the
nineteenth century, the Tiger Lily has been cultivated in
eastern Asia for over a thousand years as a food crop, and
in Kamchatka the bulbs of a native species scarcely known
as garden plants are used in soup or as a porridge.

Lilies and herbalism

In view of the fact that lilies can be consumed in quantity
with, apparently, no ill effects, it is perhaps surprising that
they have also been used medicinally. Nevertheless, there
are many recommendations about their efficacy in treat-
ing a variety of complaints. Dioscorides extols the value
of a face pack made of mashed *Krinon basilikon*
(*L. candidum*) bulbs with honey, for it "cleareth ye faces
and makes them without wrinkles" (Goodyer's translation,
1655), while the leaves were said to be an antidote to
snake bites.

14

John Gerard, in his oft-quoted *Herball* of 1597, made a far-reaching claim for the bulb-and-honey poultice: "It gleweth togither sinewes that be cut insunder." Much later, in *The New Family Herbal* of 1790, William Meyrick expanded the range of ailments for which the bulbs of the White Lily could be used: "The root bruised and applied to hard tumours softens and ripens them sooner than almost any other application. Made into an ointment they take away corns, and remove the pain and inflammation arising from pains and scalds."

It is interesting to note that the nineteenth-century herbalist-physicians such as William Woodville (author of *Medical Botany*, 1832) were still referring to *L. candidum* as the White Lily, the name Madonna being apparently unknown to them.

Epilepsy, internal parasites, lung infections, and tumors were all cases for lily treatment, but it seems that species other than the Madonna Lily were not used. Gerard did, however, acknowledge that God would not have created anything as beautiful as *L. martagon* to be without a use, it was just that the use had not been found!

Lilium album
*This etching by Nicholas Robert from his DIVERS FLEURS (1675) is of the White Lily (*L. candidum*). Records indicate that the bulbs of this species have been used medicinally from as early as the first century A.D.*

15

LILIES IN ART

THE LOVELY LILY, IN ITS VARIOUS GUISES, must surely rate as one of the most frequently illustrated plants. The earliest representations of lilies are from the ancient civilizations of Egypt and the Mediterranean. Recent finds at Thera, an island adjacent to Crete and thought by some to be the legendary Atlantis, show that the scarlet-flowered Greek native *L. chalcedonicum* was held in high esteem as a subject for artists, possibly as early as 2000 B.C.

The Minoans used *L. candidum* to decorate frescoes, and pottery found at Knossos and Amnisos in Crete dates from about 1500 B.C. The same species is depicted in rather stylized form on an Egyptian stone relief dating from between 650 and 500 B.C., and similar slightly earlier works are known from Nineveh, Assyria. This lily has also been identified in Roman garden paintings some 1900 years old at Pompeii and Herculaneum.

Few illustrations adorn the ancient Greek herbals such as that of Dioscorides, although the copy of his work which survives in Vienna, the *Codex Vindobonensis*, does contain some very good drawings added by a Byzantine artist in about A.D. 500.

Paintings in which the Madonna Lily appears abound in fifteenth-century art, but it was used earlier than this as a design in stylized form. It features in a thirteenth-century mosaic in Florence, for example, and in the eleventh-century the Navarre Knights are said to have fought in Spain with a lily motif embroidered on their breasts.

No doubt it was the ease with which *L. candidum* could be cultivated in its native Mediterranean region, and the purity of its flowers, which led to its popularity among painters of religious scenes: it was especially incorporated in depictions of the Virgin. Examples of fifteenth-century work include a superbly accurate drawing of *L. candidum* by Leonardo da Vinci, perhaps the basis for the lily in his *Annunciation* in the Uffizi Gallery, Florence. Van Eyck's *The Mystic Lamb* in Ghent Cathedral shows the Angel Gabriel holding a stem of *L. candidum*, and the Virgin's diadem is adorned with single flowers of it among jewels and pearls. An abundance of these flowers appears in Lippi's *Coronation of the Virgin* (*c.* 1447).

L. candidum
A drawing of L. candidum *by Leonardo da Vinci, perhaps the basis for the lily in his* Annunciation *in the Uffizi Gallery, Florence.*

17

The orange *L. bulbiferum* appears in a vase with an iris in the Nativity scene of the Portinari altarpiece by Hugo van der Goes (*c*. 1475, Uffizi Gallery, Florence).

The seventeenth-century Flemish flower painters lavished their talents on bulbous plants. The *Bouquet of Flowers in a Pottery Vase* by Jan Brueghel the Elder (*c*. 1599, Kunsthistorisches Mueum, Vienna) is a typical early example, with a surfeit of irises, tulips, snowdrops, cyclamen, narcissus, fritillaries, hyacinths, and three lilies (*L. martagon*, *L. bulbiferum*, and *L. chalcedonicum*).

By the eighteenth century, the botanical artists had much more scope for recording the minute detail of new floral finds. One of the great artists of the period, Georg Ehret (1708-70), was commissioned by Dr C. J. Trew of Nuremberg to paint the flowers now seen in European gardens, including *L. superbum*, recently introduced from North America.

1787 saw the publication of the first volume of Curtis's *Botanical Magazine* which was to continue as an unbroken series to the present day and in which nearly fifty species of lily have been depicted. Many of these illustrations are of great historical value since they provide a record of the individual plants upon which botanists of the day based their descriptions and names.

If lilies and botanical art are mentioned together, then the name of Pierre-Joseph Redouté must be included, for his eight-volume work *Les Liliacées*, published between 1802 and 1816, is truly a milestone in the study of lilies. However, they are treated in a very broad sense and the work displays not only the true lilies but a host of other monocotyledonous plants, even bananas and pineapples!

In 1877-80, Henry John Elwes published his folio-sized monograph of the genus *Lilium*, a beautiful work with fifty plates of the lilies then known to be in cultivation prepared by Walter Hood Fitch. One of the finest botanical artists of the time, Fitch also prepared an amazing 3000 plates for the *Botanical Magazine*. The discovery of new species since that time has led to nine supplements to the monograph, illustrated with paintings by Lilian Snelling and, more recently, by Margaret Stones.

BOUQUET OF FLOWERS IN A POTTERY VASE 1599
By Jan Brueghel the Elder (1568-1625)
[Kunsthistorisches Museum, Vienna]
*This quintessential Flemish painting
of flowering bulbs, shows three lilies*
L. martagon, L. bulbiferum, *and* L. chalcedonicum
*together with irises, tulips, snowdrops, cyclamen, narcissus,
fritillaries, and hyacinths.*

A field trial of "Asiatic hybrids" in Oregon.

THE MODERN GARDEN LILY

"But such are the monstrous devices of some fantasticall spirits, that they invented forsooth a new kind of artificiall colouring and dying of Lillies . . . they infuse them and steepe them in the lees of deep red wine."

PLINY, *HISTORY OF THE WORLD* (HOLLAND'S TRANSLATION 1601).

FORTUNATELY, THANKS TO THE SKILL of the lily breeders of the twentieth century, it is unnecessary to add to the color range using artificial means. Lilies are now available in practically any color, shape, and size for a variety of different purposes.

Systematic hybridization of lilies began in the latter part of the last century but is primarily a phenomenon of the twentieth century. There are older hybrids – for example the lovely *L. x testaceum* is a *L. candidum x L. chalcedonicum* cross from about 1812 of unrecorded origin, and the Japanese were probably hybridizing *L. dauricum* with another eastern Asiatic species to produce a range of upright-flowered plants which have been referred to more recently as *L. x elegans* and *L. x maculatum.*

Some of these were brought into Europe and further crossing with *L. bulbiferum* produced *L. x hollandicum,* otherwise known as *L. umbellatum*, describing the cluster of upright flowers at the top of the stems. These, in turn, were used in the breeding of the famous "Mid-Century hybrids" at the bulb farms of Jan de Graaff in Oregon.

Another species involved was *L. lancifolium*, giving a range of flower shapes and varying from pendent to upright. "Enchantment" was one of the earliest to be offered commercially and is still an immensely popular lily for the garden and as a cut flower. However, there are many others and new varieties of these "Asiatic hybrids," as they are officially called, appear every year in the catalogs. Other species have been introduced into the breeding of these so that their make-up is now quite complex. In view of their very varied flower shapes, some of these hybrids come into the "group 2" lilies (see page 34) and others into "group 3" (page 42).

Another group of lilies which has received the attention of breeders is that of the trumpet lily. The first hybrids, in the early twentieth century, were developments of the fragrant white trumpet species, but de Graaff, using several of these, including *L. leucanthum centifolium* and *L. sargentiae*, introduced colors not seen before in the species so that we now have a choice of white, yellow, orange, or pink, with a staining of green to brown or purple on the outside.

The orange Turk's-cap-shaped *L. henryi* has also been crossed with the trumpet lilies to add further to the variation, giving wide-open flowers with reflexed tips to the segments. 'Bright Star' is a noteworthy example. Although the Oregon Bulb Farms have carried out much of the development work with *L. henryi*, it was first crossed with *L. sargentiae* by Monsieur Debras of Orleans in France and the offspring christened *L. x aurelianense* from the ancient name for the city, Aurelia.

The Oriental lilies have also been developed by hybridization and some of the resulting plants are among the most astonishing of all. The first work was carried out in Boston by the historian Francis Parkman, who crossed the two Japanese species *L. auratum* and *L. speciosum*, obtaining a plant which was named *L. x parkmanni*. Further development by the U.S. Department of Agriculture in Beltsville, by de Graaff, and by others in Australia and New Zealand, has provided some wonderful late-summer fragrant lilies with reflexed or flattish flowers, such as 'Journey's End', 'Stargazer,' and the amazing pure-white 'Casablanca'.

There are many other breeding lines which have not been listed here, but the examples mentioned above and those shown on the following pages will give an idea of the enormous scope in this lovely group of plants, and perhaps a hint that there are endless possibilities for the hybridizer.

CHAPTER II

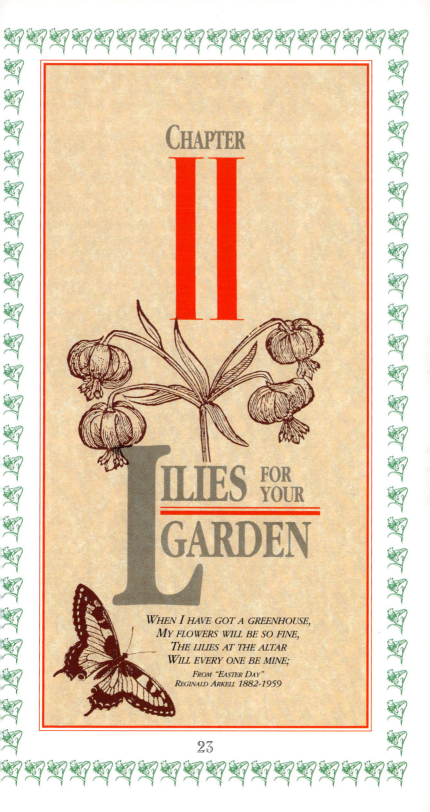

LILIES FOR YOUR GARDEN

WHEN I HAVE GOT A GREENHOUSE,
MY FLOWERS WILL BE SO FINE,
THE LILIES AT THE ALTAR
WILL EVERY ONE BE MINE;

FROM *"EASTER DAY"*
REGINALD ARKELL 1882-1959

LILIES FOR YOUR GARDEN

With a large genus such as *Lilium*, with about one hundred species, it is essential for reference purposes to group them in some way, so for this book they are arranged according to the most visually striking feature, that of the flower shape and poise.

The flowers of all lilies have the same basic structure, with six tepals, or perianth segments, six stamens, and one style, so that within the constraints of this delightful simplicity there is a limit to the possible number of variations in overall appearance. The six segments are placed so that they form a funnel or trumpet shape, open outwards to a wide cup, chalice shape or flattish flower, or are reflexed, forming the so-called Turk's-cap shape. The flowers can be held in an upright, pendent or horizontal position; the last of these is often referred to as "outward-facing."

These features combine to distinguish the four broad groups adopted in this chapter:

Group one
TRUMPET-SHAPED LILIES
(see page 28), with the flowers trumpet-shaped and horizontal or drooping.

Group two
TURK'S-CAP-SHAPED LILIES
(see page 34), with reflexed segments and pendent.

Group three
UPRIGHT CUP-SHAPED LILIES
(see page 42), with the flowers erect and cup-shaped or flattish.

Group four
THE ORIENTAL LILIES
(see page 46), containing *L. auratum*, *L. speciosum*, *L. henryi*, and their hybrids is perhaps less obvious, but they are placed together because their showy flattish-to-reflexed flowers have prominent projections or papillae on the segments.

24

WHAT IS A LILY?

Lilies belong to the part of the flowering kingdom known as monocotyledons, together with many other familiar plants such as orchids, palm trees, grasses, irises, onions, and daffodils. The seeds of these have only one seed leaf, or cotyledon, whereas the dicotyledons such as peas and cabbages have two. The monocotyledons are divided into families, one of which is the *Liliaceae*, and this in turn is split into genera such as *Lilium*, which contains the true lilies. Some of the related genera are mentioned on page 50.

LILY SEED CASES

L. martagon

L. formosanum

MCMXCII

Seed capsules
If the lily flower has been pollinated, and the ovary fertilized by the pollen, large capsules will develop that are eventually held stiffly upright. They split lengthways when ripe and, when shaken by the wind, shed numerous flat seeds which are further distributed by the wind. One capsule may contain well over 100 seeds, and one plant may have 20-30 flowers, so seed production in lilies is enormous. The capsules vary considerably in shape and size from short and broad to long and narrow.

An extra set of roots which appear on the stem just above the bulb

Small bulbils in the leaf axils

Some bulbs are rhizome-like

WHAT IS A LILY?

Leaves

Lily leaves vary considerably from narrow and very numerous to few and rather short and broad. They may be scattered all the way up the stem or produced at intervals in compact whorls with sections of bare stem in between. Some species have small bulbils in the axils of the leaves.– very useful for the gardener in propagation.

Stem

The stem arises from near the center of the bulb and carries leaves for most of its length, bearing a number of flowers in a raceme at its apex. Many species have an extra set of roots which appear on the stem just above the bulb, and these help to feed the aerial shoot. These "stem-rooting" lilies (see page 57) need to be planted deeper than those without such roots.

Bulbs

Lilies are bulbous plants, the bulbs consisting of many fleshy scales attached to a basal plate from which the roots emerge. There are many types of bulb – some are rhizome-like and creep through the soil, while others produce runners or stolons with new bulbs at their tips. The color, too, may vary from white to yellow or purplish. The majority of lilies are dormant in winter and in growth in the summer, but the Madonna Lily, *L. candidum*, produces leaves in the fall and winter.

Some bulbs produce stolons

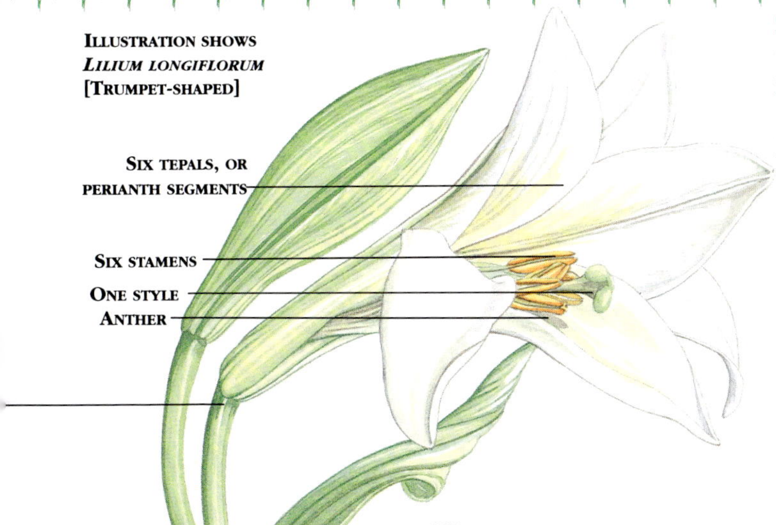

ILLUSTRATION SHOWS
LILIUM LONGIFLORUM
[TRUMPET-SHAPED]

SIX TEPALS, OR
PERIANTH SEGMENTS

SIX STAMENS
ONE STYLE
ANTHER

Flowers

Lily flowers are carried in a raceme, although this is sometimes reduced to a single flower, and sometimes they are clustered close together to give an umbel-like appearance. They may be trumpet-shaped, bell-like with reflexed tepals (these are usually known as perianth segments in monocotyledons), or flattish to cup-shaped, and may be pendent to upright. There is a great range of color from white to yellow, orange or red, and plain or variously spotted and stained with a darker color. Many lilies have a delightful fragrance.

Pollination

There are six stamens, each having a large anther which carries a heavy dusting of brown or yellow pollen. Insects, attracted by the flower color, scent, or nectar at the base of the tepals, become dusted with pollen and transfer some to the style of another flower, thus pollinating it. The fragrant white trumpet lilies are probably also pollinated at night by moths. The pollen contains a strong stain which, if brushed against, is very difficult to remove from clothes and skin.

27

TRUMPET-SHAPED LILIES

To many people the lily is epitomized by the elegant white scented trumpet types, so beloved of florists and long associated with weddings and funerals. However, not all the lilies of this group have white flowers, and by hybridization there is now, in addition to the range of lovely species, a colorful array of showy garden forms in pink, apricot, orange, yellow, and green.

'Golden Splendor'
A magnificent example of a yellow trumpet hybrid, displays huge fragrant blooms suffused with purple on the outside over varying shades of golden yellow.

LILIUM CANDIDUM
The Madonna Lily

The much-loved Madonna Lily, although included here with the trumpet lilies, is very distinct from the Asiatic species in its appearance and habit of growth. It is of eastern Mediterranean origin and has a life cycle which is in keeping with the winter-rainfall/summer-drought climate of the region, producing a set of "winter leaves" at ground level in the fall and then, in spring, a flower stem bearing rather different-looking foliage. Thus, its main period of growth is in winter and spring, whereas most lilies are winter dormant. The Madonna Lily's true distribution as a wild plant is somewhat obscured by the fact that it has long been utilized as a source of flowers and perfume by the ancient civilizations of the region. It may well have occurred much more widely than the few known localities in Greece, Israel, and Turkey where it exists today.

The early Egyptians appear to have cultivated *L. candidum* for its perfume. A small stone relief found at Memphis, and now in the Louvre Museum, Paris, depicts a group of ladies picking flowers which are believed to be lilies, probably the species we now call the Madonna Lily. This latter name, however, is a comparatively recent acquisition, possibly as late as the nineteenth century. To the Greeks it was known as *Krinon basilikon*, the Royal Lily, and in the writings of the early herbalists we can find a range of uses for various parts of the plant, from the treatment of burns to perfume for men.

L. CANDIDUM, *THE MADONNA LILY*

29

LILIUM REGALE
THE REGAL LILY

L. REGALE

It is easy to imagine the ecstasy of Ernest H. Wilson on first seeing this gorgeous trumpet-shaped, Chinese lily in the wild. At the age of 23, this Kew-trained gardener began a series of intrepid journeys in China on behalf of the nursery Veitch & Co. and the Arnold Arboretum, discovering this extraordinarily beautiful plant in August, 1903. Wilson was much impressed and waxed lyrical on the subject of its whereabouts: "onward and west-ward up the mighty Yangtsze River for 1800 miles, then northward up its tributary the Min, in narrow, semi-arid valleys, down which thunder torrents, and encompassed by mountains composed of mud shales and granites, whose peaks are clothed with snow eternal, the Regal Lily has its home." He subsequent-ly sent 300 bulbs to Veitch and further consignments to the Arnold Arboretum and, from these, countless bulbs have been raised to give pleasure to thousands. As a garden plant, its resilient wiry stems stand up well to inclement weather and it will thrive in acid or alkaline condi-tions provided that the soil is free-draining. The flowers are wonderful and will normally produce masses of seeds which form flowering bulbs in only two or three years. The large trumpets, up to ten or more per stem, are white inside and stained purple on the outside, and will fill the garden with their delightful fragrance on a still summer's evening. If asked to choose a selection of the most important plant introductions of the twentieth century, the Regal Lily would surely be among them.

L. REGALE *seen wild in its habitat in China*

THE TRUMPET-SHAPED LILIES

L. formosanum is a most graceful species, with slender trumpets that are 5-7in (12-18cm) long, white on the inside and stained wine-purple on the outside. In the early part of this century it was said to occur in hundreds of thousands in its native Taiwan (Formosa) and is still reported to be common throughout the island, growing from sea level to over 12,000ft (3600m). As a consequence of this altitude range it varies considerably in hardiness. The tall, low-altitude forms are very tender and therefore cultivated as greenhouse potted plants in cold-winter areas. The high-altitude dwarf forms will tolerate light frosts; these are known as var. *pricei* and may be only 6in (15cm) in height with one large flower per stem. *L. formosanum* flowers quickly from seed, in well under one year.

L. FORMOSANUM

L. *japonicum* has trumpets in a lovely shade of soft pink throughout. Its Japanese name means "bamboo lily," and in the wild it is associated with dwarf species of bamboo which probably give the slender wiry 3ft (1m) stems some degree of support when carrying several of the large blooms. In cultivation it needs cool growing conditions, coupled with free drainage. This lily has been used in breeding, but in conjunction with *L. auratum* and the Oriental group (see page 46) rather than in the development of trumpet-lily hybrids.

L. JAPONICUM

L. *rubellum* is in effect a miniature version of *L. japonicum,* sometimes only about 12in (30cm) in height. It is a delightful lily for a rock garden or raised peat bed. Although in the wild it is a native of cold-winter areas, its dormant bulbs are usually covered in deep snow, so have some measure of frost protection. It enjoys warm, damp summers.

L. RUBELLUM

L. longiflorum, the Easter Lily, responds well to forcing and is cultivated in quantity for the cut-flower trade early in the year, hence the common name coined for it by the English-speaking countries. Its long trumpets have a delightful fragrance and purity which make them ideal for formal floral decorations. They are a clean white both inside and out, and this is enhanced by the bright green shiny leaves. This is a very tender species and is either cultivated in warm, frost-free climates or in the protection of a greenhouse. Various selections have been made, including forms with thicker-textured flowers which travel better when transported to market. Although now cultivated on a large scale in various countries, including Bermuda from whence it has acquired the alternative name of Bermuda Lily, it is in fact a very restricted species in the wild, possibly confined to the Ryukyu Islands.

L. sargentiae is a Chinese lily related to *L. regale* and was also introduced to cultivation by E. H. Wilson. It is just as beautiful, but not nearly as robust as its regal relative, although it has the distinguishing and useful feature of producing many bulbils in the axils of its somewhat broader leaves. The gardener will also appreciate the extension of the white-trumpet-flowering season which this lily provides, for it is usually some two or three weeks later than *L. regale.*

L. leucanthum var. *centifolium* is a superb white Chinese trumpet lily which has been used in breeding programs, notably by Jan de Graaff in Oregon, together with *L. sargentiae* and some other related species, to produce the extraordinary range of cultivars available today.

L. LONGIFLORUM, *THE EASTER LILY*

L. SARGENTIAE

L. LEUCANTHUM *VAR.* CENTIFOLIUM

THE TRUMPET HYBRIDS

From the treasure house of hybrids, it is possible to give only a small selection of the wide range available. Although the first crosses were made in the early part of the twentieth century, it is to the expertise of the staff of the Oregon Bulb Farms of Jan de Graaff that we owe thanks for many of the wonderful garden lilies of today. Since the batches of seedlings which are raised vary, these are usually seen in catalogs as "strains." Within a strain the plants will have similar although not identical characteristics.

'BLACK DRAGON'

'Black Dragon' is a huge robust lily up to 6ft 6in (2m) in height, with many large trumpets which are in fact white, but shaded a rich dark maroon on the outside. 'Green Magic,' too, is white on the inside, with a hint of yellowy-green in the throat, but a cool chartreuse-green shade on the outside. Of the range of yellow trumpet hybrids, which are the result of a complex series of crosses between the white-flowered species and the orange-yellow *L. henryi*, 'Golden Splendor' (see page 28), is a good example. Its huge fragrant blooms are suffused with purple on the outside over varying shades of golden yellow. For a pink trumpet there is none better than 'Pink Perfection,' which was raised as a result of a painstaking process of selection from crosses between two white-flowered species which only showed a hint of pink coloration at first.

'GREEN MAGIC'

'PINK PERFECTION'

33

TURK'S-CAP-SHAPED LILIES

THE TURK'S-CAP-SHAPED LILIES are a varied group of species, some of them botanically unrelated to each other and with diverse origins, from Europe, Asia, and North America. It is convenient to place them together here since they all have pendent flowers, mostly smaller than those of the trumpet lilies, with their six tepals or perianth segments reflexed or rolled back, giving them a characteristic and very elegant appearance.

L. pardalinum
This striking species from the western United States does not require very moist garden conditions and will thrive in humus-rich soil.

L. *amabile* is a pleasing little Korean lily, with its red, black-spotted, Turk's-caps on slender stems, but it scarcely merits the name of *amabile* (lovely) since there are many other lilies which far exceed it in beauty. For those who prefer the species to the showy hybrids it has undoubted appeal, both in its typical red form and the yellow version, var. *luteum*. It is hardy and not at all difficult to cultivate, given good drainage and not too much shade.

L. AMABILE *VAR* LUTEUM

L. *cernuum* is an eastern Asiatic Turk's-cap which is rather short-lived and less striking, with pinkish-lilac flowers spotted dark purple. The flowers have a delightful fragrance.

Europe has its dramatic red Turk's-caps in the form of L. *chalcedonicum*. Being a native of mainland Greece, Euboea, and the Peloponnese, this lily was well known to the ancients and is illustrated in Minoan artwork. The species came to western Europe in the time of Queen Elizabeth I of England, and was referred to by John Parkinson in 1629 as "the Red Martagon of Constantinople," although its name is derived from the neighboring district of Chalcedon. The brilliant red flowers have a gloss which makes them especially striking, but it is the leaves which clearly distinguish this lily from the other red Turk's-caps. The upper ones are much shorter than the lower and are held upright and close to the stem as if trying to sheath it. In addition, all the leaves have a silvery margin. It is a lily of the early summer and, like so many Mediterranean plants, enjoys alkaline soils and a good deal of sun, although it has also been cultivated successfully in acid soils in partial shade.

L. CERNUUM

L. CHALCEDONICUM

L. DAVIDII

L. DUCHARTREI

L. HANSONII

L. davidii is a colorful and hardy Chinese Turk's-cap with bright-orange flowers spotted with black. There are up to twenty of them on 3-5ft (1-1.5m) stems which are clothed with many leaves, but these are narrow, so it appears a very graceful lily in spite of its size. It is named after the French naturalist and missionary Armand David, who made many valuable discoveries and plant introductions. A species of deer also bears his name.

L. duchartrei produces stolons which wander at random under the soil and you can never be quite sure where the lilies will appear the next year. It is at its best in dappled shade in leaf-mold-rich soil. Reginald Farrer, the great alpine gardener, explorer, and author, described its habitat in Gansu province of China as "steep shingly banks of loam and light coppice," and likened the flower color to "cold bone-white," although the whiteness is relieved by purple spots and streaks, prompting him to refer to it as the Marble Martagon.

The interesting *L. hansonii* is named not after an intrepid traveller or botanist, but commemorates an amateur gardening enthusiast of the genus, Peter Hanson of New York. Although readily obtainable in the nursery trade, and an excellent garden plant which is very easy to grow in humus-rich soil in dappled shade, this lily is very restricted in the wild and occurs naturally only on Take-shima Island between Japan and Korea. It is clearly related to the true Martagon Lily and has similar whorls of leaves on its stem. However, it differs strikingly in having fragrant orange-yellow flowers spotted brown, and the segments are of a thick waxy texture.

L. lancifolium (*L. tigrinum*)
is the Tiger Lily from eastern Asia,
but exactly why it bears this name
is obscure. The flowers are orange
with dark spots and look more
leopard-like than tiger-striped.
Although a striking lily, its first
claim to fame appears to have
been as a food for eastern Asiatic
peoples over a thousand years
ago: the starch-rich bulbs reputed-
ly taste like mashed potatoes. It
was not until 1804 that bulbs
reached Europe, when a consign-
ment arrived at Kew Gardens.
Blackish bulbils are produced in
the leaf axils, making it easy to
propagate, so it has been a fairly
common lily in gardens
ever since.

   L. langkongense is a rare plant
in its wild habitat in Yunnan
province of western China, but is
a firm favorite among lily fanciers
and has been used to great effect
in hybridization. Its 20-40in (0.5-
1m) stems bear several quite large
pale-pink Turk's-cap flowers with
markedly pointed segments,
giving it a graceful and distinctive
appearance.

   The Japanese *L. leichtlinii* is
seldom seen in gardens, but its
variety *maximowiczii* is cultivated
and is a far easier plant to grow.
In general appearance this is very
like the Tiger Lily, with orange,
dark-spotted flowers, but its stems
do not produce bulbils and they
have the curious habit of wander-
ing underground before pushing
up into flower. The species is
named after the famous
nineteenth-century German
nurseryman, Max Leichtlin of
Baden-Baden, who specialized in
bulbous plants. The variety carries
the name of Carl Maximowicz,
a renowned Russian botanist of
the period.

L. LANCIFOLIUM (L.TIGRINUM)

L. LANGKONGENSE

L. LEICHTLINII

L. MARTAGON

L. MONADELPHUM

L. NEPALENSE

THE TURK'S-CAP SHAPE

The true Turk's-cap, *L. martagon,* is a modest European species, very hardy, and a lily of quiet charm which is best used in gardens for planting in a lightly wooded semi-naturalized setting. Its 5-6ft 6in (1.5-2m) stems carry up to fifty small pinkish flowers with darker spots, and there are also attractive white (var. *album*) and very dark purple variants. The curious name may have some connection with Mars, for in medieval times plants which were of medicinal value were considered to be under the influence of one of the stars or planets. Martagon may be derived from Marti-genus, "child of Mars."

L. szovitsianum and *L. mon-adelphum* may be likened to giant Turk's-caps, Caucasian species which are so similar that it is unnecessary to grow both except for botanical curiosity. The large soft-yellow pendent bells reflex their segments gracefully, usually about five to ten of them on stout stems up to 3ft (1m) in height, and they are pleasantly fragrant. Both species do well in heavier soils enriched with leaf mold for they are plants of mountain woodlands in the wild.

L. nepalense, although Himalayan, is a tender species for a sheltered border, or cool greenhouse in colder areas. It needs space to wander, for the bulbs produce stoloniferous stems. In flower shape it is somewhat between the trumpet and Turk's-cap shape, but the flowers are pendent and the segments recurve gracefully, so it fits quite well into this group. Its coloring is remarkable – the bells are a rich greenish-yellow outside but stained deep maroon on the inside, except for the reflexed tips which are the same greeny-yellow shade.

The spectacular *L. pomponium* is the scarlet Martagon of the Maritime Alps. This lily does best in warm chalky soils. It is a most delightful plant, with up to ten or more sealing-wax red flowers spotted with black, on 16-24in (40-60cm) stems which are densely clothed with narrow leaves. Such beauty has been long appreciated in gardens, for it was described by Clusius in 1601.

Rather similar in its pendent red flowers is the much better known *L. pumilum (L. tenuifolium)*, which is smaller and daintier still, with very narrow grassy leaves on wiry stems only 16-20in (40-50cm) tall. There may be up to twenty of the fragrant sealing-wax red flowers, which are unspotted. It is said that in its natural home in China and Tibet the local people plant the bulbs in the mud roofs of their houses. The message to gardeners is that this lily likes good drainage! Although a short-lived plant, it is easily raised from seed and will flower in only a year or two from sowing. 'Golden Gleam' is an equally attractive deep-yellow form.

L. pyrenaicum is a native of the Pyrenees mountains and has smallish Turk's-cap-shaped flowers which may be red, although in its common form they are greenish-yellow, dotted and streaked with black towards the center. This lily is easily cultivated and is suitable for naturalizing in grass or between shrubs, but is not greatly appreciated since the plant is rather large and leafy compared with the size of its flowers. These have a distinctly unpleasant smell, but a well-grown specimen with about ten flowers looks quite striking. It is certainly not a lily to be despised since it is very hardy and the first of the season in early summer.

L. POMPONIUM

L. PUMILUM (L.TENUIFOLIUM)

L. PYRENAICUM

L. SUPERBUM, *SWAMP LILY*

L. PARDALINUM, *PANTHER LILY*

L. CANADENSE

NORTH AMERICAN TURK'S-CAPS

Although similar in flower shape to the Old World members of this group, the North American lilies have a rather different bulb structure and, in addition, those mentioned here prefer damp conditions.

L. superbum, the Swamp Lily, thrives in boggy meadows and marshy places. It is aptly named superbum, for the stems can be up to 10ft (3m) in height, carrying neat whorls of leaves and up to forty large flowers with elegantly pointed segments, orange with darker reddish tips and a greenish star in the center.

The bulbs of *L. superbum,* and the similar Panther Lily, *L. pardalinum* (see page 34), from the western States have many smallish scales attached to a thick rhizome which builds up into large colonies. They thrive in a humus-rich soil, provided that it does not dry out in the summer months. The Panther Lily has heavily spotted flowers, the centers being blotched and speckled purple on a yellow-orange ground, shading to red in the upper half of the segments. It pays to plant the bulbs fairly near the surface.

One of the most graceful of all lilies, *L.canadense* is very widespread in the eastern United States as well as eastern Canada. It was probably introduced into Europe by the French in the early seventeenth century, but is not a common garden plant in spite of being hardy and easily cultivated. The elegant bell-shaped flowers with their outward-curving segments may be yellow to orange or red, usually spotted inside with dark purple. However, some forms of this lily are unspotted.

HYBRID TURK'S-CAPS

There are now many superb garden hybrids available as a result of breeding programs which began in the 1920s and have continued through to the present day. The parentage is complicated and involves many species, but those which have contributed to the hybrids with pendent Turk's-cap flowers include *L. davidii*, *L. lancifolium*, *L. cernuum*, *L. leichtlinii*, and *L. amabile*.

'Citronella Strain,' one of the Jan de Graaff hybrids from Oregon, produces a mass of lemon to deep-yellow blooms spotted with brown and with prominent deep-orange stamens. The showy and very popular 'Bright Star,' although placed here because of its flower shape, is not related to this group and has originated from crosses between the white trumpet lilies and orange *L. henryi* (see page 47), a species with reflexed segments bearing very prominent hair-like papillae on the surface, which are also to be seen in 'Bright Star.' This lily has creamy flowers with an orange star in the center.

In addition to the delightful North American species, some excellent hybrids between them have been raised, the most famous of which are the "Bellingham Hybrids," developed by the U.S. Department of Agriculture at Bellingham in the state of Washington in the first half of the twentieth century. Many of these variable hybrids were selected out and given distinguishing names, but few are now to be found except for 'Shuksan,' which is a magnificent vigorous lily with large orange-yellow flowers conspicuously blotched dull red.

'CITRONELLA STRAIN'

'BRIGHT STAR'

'SHUKSAN'

UPRIGHT, CUP-SHAPED LILIES

T HIS GROUP OF LILIES has upright, or outward-facing, cup-shaped to flattish flowers and contains a few species which are quite similar to each other. Many specimens from this "shape group" have been used by plant breeders to raise a magnificent array of showy and very easily cultivated lilies for our gardens.

L. bulbiferum, the Orange Lily, is a typical species of this group and is rather widespread in the European mountains from the Pyrenees eastwards through the Alps to Hungary. Its reddish-orange flowers are in the form of upturned cups, spotted darker and furnished with warty protuberances inside. Normally this lily has no stem bulbils in the leaf axils, but the variety *croceum* does usually produce these, and has orange flowers without the reddish tint. Although perhaps not as graceful as the elegant trumpet or pendent-flowered lilies, these upright lilies are blessed with a tough constitution and have been cultivated since at least the sixteenth century.

L. concolor is a delicate-looking Chinese species which, although quite hardy, is rather shorter lived. This is not a problem, however, since new stocks are fairly easy to raise from seed. The lily grows up to 3ft (1m) in height with narrow scattered leaves. Its slender stem is crowned by a cluster of up to ten erect flattish flowers in brilliant unspotted scarlet. There are also spotted variants such as var. *pulchellum*.

L. BULBIFERUM

L. dauricum *(left)*

This is a Siberian species and, through a misunderstanding of its origin, was at first given the name of "L. pennsylvanicum." It is a stocky plant, up to about 28in (70cm) in height, with several upturned widely cup-shaped flowers in varying shades of red to orange, spotted inside with darker brown. It is an easily cultivated lily which prefers a sunny position. It is very hardy, so has proved an excellent parent for many of the hybrids with upward-facing flowers.

L. CONCOLOR

'CHINOOK'

'CONNECTICUT KING'

'COTE D'AZUR'

UPRIGHT, CUP-SHAPED HYBRIDS

L. maculatum is a variable plant, perhaps of hybrid origin and resulting from crosses made long ago in Japan between *L. dauricum* and *L. concolor*. The flowers are upturned and cup-shaped in a great range of colors from yellow through orange to red, spotted or unspotted. After their introduction into Europe in the early nineteenth century, further breeding took place involving *L. bulbiferum,* leading to the development of the *L. x hollandicum* hybrids, often known in gardens as "*L. umbella-tum*" because of the umbel-like clusters of flowers at the top of the stems. These are now largely superseded by the wonderful modern hybrids developed initially by Jan de Graaff in the 1950s, and appropriately given the group name of "Mid-Century Hybrids." Some of the individually named cultivars are described here, but the range is enormous and growing year by year.

'Chinook' was raised by de Graaff's Oregon Bulb Farms and introduced in 1972. It has pale apricot-colored flowers, dark-spotted in the center.

'Connecticut King' is the most well known of a wide range of hybrids raised by D. M. Stone and F. H. Payne in the 1960s and 1970s with Connecticut as part of the name. This bright-yellow unspotted lily is an excellent garden plant and is often to be found in florists as a cut flower.

'Cote d'Azur' is a modern Dutch hybrid in a lovely shade of rose red, lightly spotted darker in the center.

'ENCHANTMENT'

'Enchantment' is one of the original "Mid-Century Hybrids" and is still rated as one of the best. It is excellent in the garden, as a potted plant, and as a cut flower. The upturned flowers are orange-red, black-spotted in the center, and are produced fairly early in the summer-lily season.

'Feuerzauber' is, as its name suggests, a glowing reddish-orange, a very showy Dutch hybrid of the 1970s.

'Sterling Star' is a most attractive white lily. The flattish upward-facing flowers are white with dark spots and contrasting dark-brown stamens. It is another of the superb hybrids from the Oregon Bulb Farms.

'FEUERZAUBER'

'STERLING STAR'

45

THE ORIENTAL LILIES

THE THREE LILIES IN THIS GROUP are placed together because they have flattish to reflexed flowers which have very prominent hair-like papillae protruding from the inner surfaces of their perianth segments. They have been hybridized to produce a range of extremely showy fragrant lilies that flower late in the season and include some of the largest blooms of all. Two of the species are Japanese and the third Chinese, hence the name "Oriental" for this group.

'Journey's End'
A beautiful and colorful Oriental hybrid, with several large deep-crimson flowers, edged and tipped with white and spotted with a darker maroon inside.

L. auratum, the Golden-rayed Lily of Japan, long known to the Japanese as a spectacular garden plant, was not introduced to western horticulture until 1862 when, according to John Lindley, "ten thousand eyes beheld it at South Kensington" at one of the Royal Horticultural Society's shows. It appears that only ten days later it was also exhibited, as a result of a completely separate introduction, at the Massachusetts Horticultural Society, so it seems likely that there was an informal race in progress to spring this lily upon the public. The fact that the gardening world was stunned is not surprising, for this is a truly magnificent plant with saucer-shaped flowers about 12in (30cm) across. They are white, spotted with crimson, and have a yellow band along the center of each segment. As if this is not enough, the blooms also have a delightful fragrance. As a garden plant this is a hardy lily, requiring plenty of moisture with excellent drainage in the growing season, ideally with the base of the stem shaded and protected by dwarf shrubs or herbaceous plants and the upper parts in full sun.

Professor Augustine Henry was employed as a medical officer in the Chinese Customs Service, but was also an ardent plant collector who sent bulbs of his new discovery to Kew Gardens in 1889. *L. henryi* is a very distinctive lily, with tall purplish stems up to 8ft (2.5m) in height, carrying rather broad shiny green leaves and several orange flowers on long horizontal stalks. The segments are rolled back, leaving the stamens projecting very prominently and clearly displaying the many tiny papillae which cover the lower surfaces. This is a very hardy and easily cultivated lily.

L. AURATUM

L. HENRYI

L. SPECIOSUM

ORIENTAL LILIES

'CASA BLANCA'

'JOURNEY'S END'

'STARGAZER'

L. speciosum (see previous page) is a Japanese species which most certainly deserves the epithet "*speciosum*" (showy), a well-grown specimen surely being one of the most striking of all lilies. The reflexed white or pale-pink segments have attractive wavy edges and are stained and spotted with carmine near the base. The many long protruding papillae add to its character. This lily was noted by the botanist Kaempfer in the late seventeenth century, but was not introduced to western horticulture until the 1830s when bulbs were sent to Ghent Botanical Gardens by von Siebold. It is slightly tender for cold areas and flowers so late in the season that it is liable to be damaged by early frosts. However, it is an excellent potted plant for a large conservatory and its hybrid offspring are hardier.

Oriental hybrids

'Casa Blanca' (top left) is a recent Dutch hybrid derived from earlier *L. auratum x L. speciosum* crosses, having pure-white fragrant flowers some 10-12in (25-30cm) in diameter, flattish with recurved tips to the segments and with contrasting purple-brown stamens. It is a very vigorous grower and superb in pots.

'Journey's End' (center) was raised in New Zealand and is another *L. auratum x L. speciosum* cross with several semi-pendent, large, deep-crimson flowers, edged and tipped with white and spotted darker maroon inside.

'Stargazer' is unusual in this group in having its flowers facing upwards on short stems, so is particularly showy and often used for cultivation in pots. The flowers are almost entirely crimson except for narrow pale margins to the segments with darker spotting within.

'Black Beauty' is one of the few really successful hybrids between *L. speciosum* and *L. henryi*. It is a superb plant which is as vigorous now as when it was raised and introduced by Leslie Woodriff nearly forty years ago. It has pendent, very dark maroon-red flowers with a green star in the center and the segments roll back gracefully. There are sometimes as many as thirty blooms on a 6ft 6in (2m) stem.

'Black Beauty'

An unusual lily, L. MACKLINIAE

The very unusual L. mackliniae was discovered in seed on the border between Burma and Manipur by Frank Kingdon-Ward while searching for crashed American aircraft in 1946. What a surprise it must have been when it flowered in England at Wisley Garden two years later, for its white bell-like flowers are quite unlike those of any other lily.

49

C. GIGANTEUM

NOMOCHARIS PARDANTHINA

NOTHOLIRION CAMPANULATUM

SOME LILY RELATIVES

Cardiocrinum
The Giant Lily is a close relative of the true lilies and, apart from its colossal size, differs most obviously in having large heart-shaped leaves. The most well-known species, *C. giganteum*, is aptly named, for its white trumpets are about 6in (15cm) long and the overall height can be as much as 13ft (4m). The bulbs die after flowering, but produce offsets which eventually also flower. There are several species from the Himalayan region and eastern Asia.

Nomocharis
Although very similar to the lilies in their habit of growth, these beautiful Chinese relatives differ in that they mostly have flattish flowers with the inner petals broader than the outer and often fringed along the margins. The flowers are dramatically blotched or zoned, with a deeper color inside. There are about eight species in China, Burma, and Tibet, one of the most striking of which is *N. pardanthina*.

Notholirion
This small group of attractive lily-like plants have very different bulbs encased in brown tunics. The leaves are rather long and narrow, and the funnel-shaped flowers are generally smaller than those of the lilies. The bulbs die after flowering, but bulblets are produced to carry on the next generation. The six species are to be found in the Himalayan region and China. Shown here is *N. campanulatum*.

50

Chapter

III

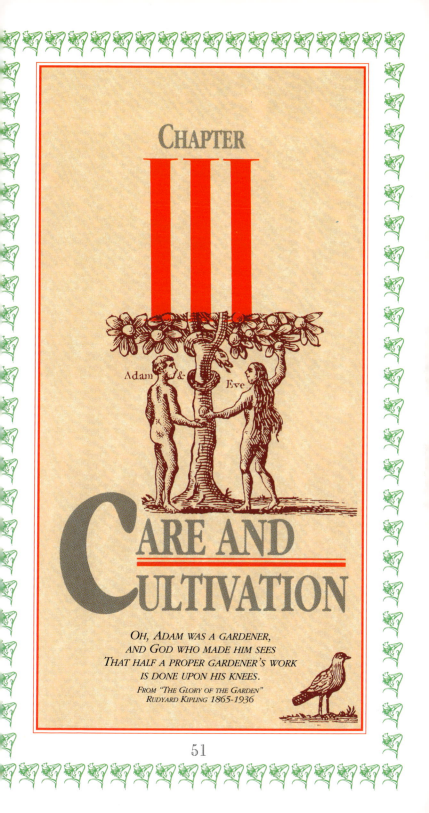

Adam & Eve

Care and Cultivation

Oh, Adam was a gardener,
and God who made him sees
That half a proper gardener's work
is done upon his knees.

From "The Glory of the Garden"
Rudyard Kipling 1865-1936

BUYING BULBS

THE AMATEUR GARDENER is entirely dependent upon the lily growers and retailers when it comes to choosing the time to purchase and plant new lilies. The grower, in turn, depends upon the growth cycle of the lily, and the time of marketing is governed by the plants themselves, which do not die down until the fall. Some lilies do not even flower until late summer or early fall, so cannot be moved before this and must be handled before the spring, when they begin to grow again. There are, therefore, two main periods when lily bulbs are on sale – in late fall and again in early spring. An exception is *L. candidum*, which begins to grow in early fall, and is usually on sale much earlier than other species.

The ideal time to plant lily bulbs is as soon as possible

after they have been lifted from the nursery in the fall, so that the roots and bulbs do not dry out and shrivel, providing the maximum amount of time for them to become established before the winter sets in. Some nursery owners sell their bulbs in the fall, while others lift them and put them in controlled cold storage until the spring. It is best to obtain the bulbs as soon as they are on the market, be it fall or spring, and plant them immediately. With fall planting, if the soil has become frosty, it may be necessary to pot up the bulbs and keep them in a cool place, just frost-free and slightly watered, until spring when they can be planted out in their allotted positions. These pots need not be much larger than the bulbs, since they will hold the bulbs only a short time.

Displaying lilies
Some lilies, such as the newer varieties, are always expensive – you may be able to buy only one bulb of each – but generally it is better to plant in groups of three or more to give a good display. Seen here, from left to right, are 'Golden Splendor,' 'Emerald Strain,' 'Black Dragon,' and 'Pink Perfection.'

Choosing bulbs
Choose firm bulbs with plump roots attached, avoiding shrivelled or dry bulbs, and discarding any that show signs of rotting around the base. Also reject any bulbs that show much physical damage to the scales, and any that have small patches of blue mold, since the latter may get worse when you plant the bulbs out.

Site, soil, & planting

MOST LILIES DO WELL if planted where their bulbs will be shaded by low-growing shrubs or perennials, or sited in the dappled shade of taller shrubs and trees, so that their stems poke through into the sunlight.

Soil preparation

Before planting it is well worth preparing the site by deep digging. Remove one whole spade's depth of soil and put it to one side, then dig in a liberal amount of well-rotted organic matter, preferably containing a good proportion of leaf mold. Do not use fresh manure. If the drainage is poor, add sharp sand or even a coarser gravel if necessary, but avoid making a sump of the lily-planting site into which all the water will drain. You may find it necessary to raise the planting area slightly above the surrounding soil to prevent this. Also work in some general NPK (nitrogen, phosphorus, potassium)-balanced fertilizer. The top layer of soil should also be enriched with organic matter and the same fertilizer, plus sand if necessary, before you fill in on top of the lily bulbs.

Spacing and planting

For the larger-growing lilies, allow a space of about 1ft (30cm) across for a single bulb; for three bulbs planted in a triangle, a 2ft (60cm) diameter hole should suffice. Smaller species such as *L. pumilum* may be planted much closer, at 4-6in (10-15cm) apart. The planting depth needs to be about 6-8in (15-20cm) for large bulbs and 4-6in (10-15cm) for the smaller ones. *L. candidum* is again an exception, and the bulbs of this lily should be planted with their tips just below soil level. If the bulbs have good roots attached, spread these out before covering them with soil. In a well-prepared site with good drainage it should not be necessary to place more sand around the bulb, but if you are doubtful it might be as well to encase the bulb in a thin layer of gritty sand.

Before filling in the hole it is a good idea to place a small stick or cane next to each bulb to mark its position. Later on, if the lily requires support, you can push in a large cane close to the same spot without the worry of spearing the bulb. It is also a good idea to attach a label, since you may not remember which species of lily it was you planted, and visitors to the garden will almost certainly want to know!

Most lilies can be grown on alkaline soils, provided that a liberal amount of humus is worked in at planting time, with further top dressings later on. Some species, however, are much more tolerant than others, including *L. amabile*, *L. candidum*, *L. henryi*, *L. pardalinum*, *L. cernuum*, *L. chalcedonicum*, and *L. pomponium*.

After-care

After planting, there is little to be done until the young shoots break through the soil in late spring, and it is then worth checking for forecasts of late frosts. The tender growths can be damaged, even in the case of the hardiest of lilies, so keep some loose straw at hand to scatter over them on very cold nights.

The developing plants will require a constant supply of moisture, so be prepared to water during dry periods, and also top-dress the plants with a layer of well-rotted organic matter, especially in the case of the stem-rooting lilies. Weak liquid feeds also help to maintain vigor; the fertilizers intended for tomatoes are useful since they contain a good proportion of potash, to which bulbous plants in general respond well. At all times keep an eye out for pests and diseases (see page 62) and take appropriate action if there are problems.

Tall lilies will almost certainly require staking, so replace the marker sticks with strong canes that are slightly shorter than the final height of the lilies so that they are not too obvious. Tie the stems as they develop.

After flowering, if seeds are not required, cut off the stems just below the flowers and continue to water and feed until the leaves begin to turn color in late summer or fall. When the stems and their leaves have died back they can be cut off at soil level. This is also the time to lift and divide any congested clumps, usually every two to three years if the lilies are growing well.

GROWING LILIES IN CONTAINERS

THERE ARE VARIOUS REASONS FOR GROWING LILIES in containers. They may grow better in pots than in the local soil conditions or climate. It is also a way in which the tender species can be grown in cold areas in conservatories, and even the hardy ones can be encouraged to flower earlier for decorative use under glass. In small gardens it is an excellent way in which to cultivate them for a patio or terrace and, when grown in containers, they can be placed in a prominent position when in flower and afterward moved away again to make room for something else.

The time for potting is the same as that for planting out in the garden – as soon as they can be obtained in fall or early spring. The choice of containers is extensive, both in size and in the materials they are made from, and it is really a matter of selecting which you find the most attractive. Plants in earthenware pots look good but require more watering in dry summers, while those in plastic containers may be waterlogged for long periods in wet weather. Clearly, local conditions will have some bearing on your choice. On the whole it is probably better to be in control of the watering, so clay pots or wooden tubs are ideal. As a rough guide to size, one bulb of a large lily such as *L. regale* or one of the trumpet hybrids would need a 9in (22.5cm) diameter pot, whereas the same pot would take three to five bulbs of a smaller species, for example *L. pumilum* and the Asiatic hybrids such as 'Connecticut King' and 'Sterling Star.'

The bottom of the container needs a layer of broken crocks or coarse gravel over the drainage hole to stop the soil washing through, and a layer of rough well-rotted organic matter, which will help to act as a reservoir of nutrients and moisture later on as the roots develop. The potting soil needs to be an open well-drained mix, preferably based on loam. A 1:1:1 mix of loam, leaf mold, and sharp sand works well, enriched with a general balanced fertilizer at the rate recommended by the manufacturer. Place the bulbs about two-thirds of the way down the pot and push in a small stick to mark their positions, then cover them with soil, leaving a gap of 2in (5cm) between the surface and the rim of the pot so that more soil or well-rotted compost can be added in summer; this is particularly important for those lilies which produce stem roots. The marker sticks can be replaced by stronger canes later on when the stems are more fully developed.

After planting and watering, place the containers in a cool place for the rest of the winter and early spring, preferably plunged up to their rims in sand or a similar medium to keep them at a uniform temperature and frost-free; a loose covering of straw will also help. As the top growth commences they need to be given more water and light, finally moving them to their flowering positions when there is no danger of frost at night. Large containers are difficult to handle, but a small two-wheeled "sack truck" is ideal for this purpose.

When the lilies die down in the fall, cut off the stems and either repot the bulbs if they are in fairly small containers, or top-dress them if they are in large ones. This consists of removing the old soil down to the level of the bulbs and replacing it with fresh soil. As long as the bulbs remain healthy and not too congested, they can stay for three years or more in the same containers before complete repotting becomes essential.

Lilies for container growing
Most lilies can be grown in pots, but species that are particularly good to try are L. auratum, L. cernuum, L. formosanum, L. japonicum, L. longiflorum, L. pumilum, L. regale, L. rubellum, L. sargentiae, L. speciosum, the Asiatic hybrids, the Oriental hybrids, and the trumpet hybrids. All of these are likely to produce stem roots, so require deep planting. The example shown on the right is 'Stargazer,' a trumpet hybrid.

PROPAGATION

THERE ARE THREE MAIN WAYS OF INCREASING LILIES – by division of established clumps; by bulblets or bulbils produced naturally by the plants or induced artificially by removing bulb scales; or by seed. The first method is simply a matter of lifting clumps in the fall, dividing them into single bulbs and replanting them into a freshly prepared site. Some rhizomatous bulbs, such as *L. pardalinum,* tend to form a dense mat of bulbs that may require cutting up into sections, each with a growing tip.

Propagation by bulblets, bulbils, and scales

Some lilies produce bulblets on the underground part of the stem just above the bulb, while others produce small bulbils on the aerial part of the stem in the leaf axils. These can be removed in late summer and planted into pots or boxes for overwintering in a cool frame or greenhouse for growing on during the following summer. Alternatively, they can be planted directly into a prepared "nursery bed" of fertile soil. At first they must be covered by only 1in (2.5cm) of soil, then top-dressed when in growth during the next season. These small bulbs can be brought to flowering size in just one or two years.

You can also use bulb scales to increase lilies and this is quite a simple and rapid method of building up a stock. Most lily bulbs consist of many scales, and a few of these can be broken off without harming the parent bulb at any time between mid summer and early fall; it is usually possible to scrape away the soil down to the growing bulb to do this. Then dust the scales with a fungicide and place them in a polyethylene bag of slightly damp perlite, vermiculite, or clean sharp sand in a warm room at about 70°F (21°C). In about three to five weeks you should see small bulbs forming on the broken surfaces and, when roots have formed, you can detach these and plant them in soil in pots, deep boxes, or a prepared bed. As with the naturally produced bulblets and bulbils, flowering can be achieved in a matter of one or two years, and all the offspring will be identical to the parent plants.

Propagation by seed

The advantages of increasing lilies from seed are that a large number of young bulbs can be raised from just one parent, and virus diseases are not transferred to the off-spring. On the other hand, it generally takes longer to obtain flowering-sized bulbs, and the offspring will not necessarily be the same as the parent bulb.

The simplest method is to sow the seeds thinly in a pot of well-drained soil, covering them with a thin layer of grit, as you acquire them between fall and spring. Then water the pots and place them outdoors or in a cold frame or greenhouse to germinate. In the first year of growth they are best left undisturbed and given liquid feeds. However, if they grow very strongly, the whole pot of seedlings can be potted on into a larger container, or planted out into a pre-pared seedling bed of good soil. Tender species such as *L. longiflorum* and *L. formosanum* must, of course, be kept under glass after sowing and not be placed outside until the threat of frost has passed.

The germination method of lilies is not straightforward. The seeds of some species germinate almost immediately, while others have what is known as "delayed germination": the seeds need alternating periods of heat and cold before they will germinate. Within these two groups, some lilies produce a thread-like seedling leaf above ground (epigeal germination) and others do not (hypogeal). In the latter case, the seed first produces a small bulb, which then gives rise to a much broader true leaf above ground. The seeds of all types can be sown as described above, but for quicker results it is better to treat them in different ways. Sow those that germinate immediately in early spring and keep them growing as vigorously as possible by feeding through to the fall, then repot them or plant them out. The lilies with delayed germination are best sown in the fall and kept warm, at about 70°F (21°C). Keep them in a greenhouse or indoors during the early winter months, then place them outdoors in a cold frame or plunge bed for the rest of the winter and early spring, by which time germination should have occurred; then treat them as above for the rest of the year.

Flowering and germination times

Lilies vary considerably in the length of time they take to flower from seed. The quickest is *L. longiflorum,* which can flower under glass in about six months from sowing. The Asiatic hybrids can flower in one year, and *L. regale* in two, while *L. martagon* may take four to seven years.

Lilies mentioned in this book which have almost immediate germination include *L. amabile, L. candidum* (but some seeds are often also delayed), *L. cernuum, L. concolor, L. dauricum, L. davidii, L. duchartrei, L. formosanum, L. henryi, L. langkongense, L. leichtlinii, L. leucanthum, L. longiflorum, L. mackliniae, L. x maculatum, L. nepalense, L. pumilum, L. pyrenaicum, L. regale, L. sargentiae, L. lancifolium,* and most of the Asiatic and trumpet hybrids. The delayed germination types include *L. auratum, L. bulbiferum, L. canadense, L. carniolicum, L. chalcedonicum, L. hansonii, L. japonicum, L. martagon, L. monadelphum* and *L. szovtisianum, L. pardalinum, L. pomponium, L. rubellum, L. speciosum, L. superbum,* and the Oriental hybrids.

lilium rubrum bulbiferum.

Lilium flore flauo.

FRAGRANCE IN LILIES

MANY LILIES HAVE A FRAGRANCE and this ranges from extremely powerful and pleasant to very slight, and occasionally rather unpleasant. It is the white trumpet types that are noted for their wonderful perfume, in keeping with many other plants with white petals that form a funnel or tube shape, a combination that is often associated with pollination by night-flying moths. In fact the trumpet lilies are especially fragrant in the evenings, although they are also visited by insects during the day, no doubt attracted by the perfume produced by the nectaries at the base of the petals. The purity of the Madonna Lily (*L. candidum*) is also accompanied by a most delightful scent.

By contrast, some of the very gaudily colored lilies with upright cup-shaped flowers such as *L. bulbiferum* and *L. dauricum* have very little scent or none at all – presumably, the would-be pollinators are enticed by the striking colors.

The Turk's-cap-shaped types vary greatly in their fragrance, the Tiger Lily (*L. lancifolium*) having hardly any scent at all, while others, like *L. langkongense, L. chalcedonicum,* and *L. hansonii,* have attractive and quite distinct perfumes. Some, by consensus of opinion, are definitely bad-smelling, including *L. martagon,* which has been likened to "a dead mouse by the hot-water pipes" and a "sweaty leather wrist band." *L. pomponium* and *L. pyrenaicum* are also both generally acknowledged to have a rather distasteful aroma, but there is of course no need to smell them if they are known to be unpleasant, and this is no reason to avoid planting these otherwise excellent lilies.

The Oriental-group lilies are notable for their fragrance, *L. auratum* having a heavy sweet perfume and *L. speciosum* almost as powerful, so it is not surprising that their hybrid offspring are similarly endowed.

A list of the best with regard to fragrance would have to include *L. auratum, L. candidum, L. henryi, L. langkongense, L. leucanthum centifolium, L. regale, L. sargentiae,* and *L. speciosum.*

Pests & diseases

Lilies are susceptible to the usual garden pests, such as slugs and snails, which love the young shoots and, to some extent, the bulbs. These can be controlled by hand-picking at night or by the use of proprietary slug killers, and you can discourage attacks on bulbs by encasing them in sharp sand at planting time. Aphids will cause distortion of the flowers if they attack at the bud stage; they also transmit virus diseases, so it is important to control them by spraying regularly or by rubbing them off with your finger and thumb. Some other problems you may encounter are:

Lily beetle
A problem in some areas is the bright-red lily beetle and its dirty-brown larvae, which are capable of completely defoliating lilies in summer. Remove these by hand or with insecticides.

Bulb rot
Basal rots of bulbs involve various fungal organisms that may attack bulbs in store. When planted, the symptoms sometimes show up as wilting or early dying back of the foliage. To discourage bulb rots, make sure that drainage is good and the soil not too rich in fresh organic matter. Diseased bulbs are best destroyed if they can be replaced, but if they are exceptional ones remove the diseased scales and dip the bulbs in a benomyl solution mixed according to the maker's instructions. Leave them for half an hour.

Botrytis
Lily diseases include Botrytis, which is seen as dark blotches that spread and eventually kill the entire leaf, sometimes the whole aerial stem, if left unchecked. It is at its worst in warm wet weather. Use systemic fungicides, such as those containing benomyl, as soon as you see it, or even as a routine precaution.

Virus diseases
Virus diseases can badly distort the shoots and flowers, making them unsightly, and the only course of action is to destroy the affected plants before they pass it on to other healthy lilies. Slight symptoms show up as pale mottling or streaks on the leaves and, although this may not be disfiguring enough to warrant destruction of the bulbs, the virus may be transmitted to other lilies by aphids. Viruses are not transmitted from one generation to the next by seed, so new virus-free stocks can be raised in this way.

Some nurseries offer stocks of lily bulbs which have been "cleaned" of virus by micropropagation techniques, but these can, of course, be reinfected once planted in the garden.

CLASSIFICATION OF LILIES

WITH MANY THOUSANDS OF LILY HYBRIDS it is necessary to have an internationally accepted classification. The system proposed in 1963 has worked quite well, although as the breeding programs develop the divisions become less clear. There are nine of these divisions, arranged as follows:

Division I
The Asiatic hybrids derived from species such as *L. amabile*, *L. cernuum*, *L. davidii*, *L. leichtlinii*, *L. x maculatum*, *L. pumilum*, and *L. lancifolium*; the European *L. bulbiferum* is also included. The hybrids are sub-divided into those with (a) upright, (b) outward-facing, or (c) pendent flowers.

Division II
Hybrids involving *L. martagon* or *L. hansonii*, thus having true Turk's-cap flowers with whorled leaves.

Division III
Hybrids of European species such as *L. candidum* and *L. chalcedonicum*, but excluding *L. martagon*.

Division IV
Hybrids of the American species.

Division V
Hybrids derived from *L. longiflorum* and *L. formosanum*.

Division VI
Hybrids derived from the Asiatic trumpet lilies and including the Turk's-cap *L. henryi*, but not the Japanese species, *L. auratum*, *L. speciosum*, *L. rubellum*, and *L. japonicum*. The flower shape is varied because of the inclusion of *L. henryi* in these hybrids, so there are four subdivisions based on flower shape, ranging from trumpet to bowl-shaped or flattish.

Division VII
The Oriental hybrids between *L. auratum*, *L. speciosum*, *L. japonicum*, and *L. rubellum*, plus any crosses of these with *L. henryi*.

Division VIII
A home for any hybrids not accounted for in the other divisions.

Bibliography

Many books and journals have been consulted,
and the following will be found to make useful and pleasurable reading:

Growing Lilies, Derek Fox, Croom Helm 1985
Lilies, Carl Feldmaier, Batsford 1970
Lilies and Related Flowers, Pierre-Joseph Redouté illustrations,
text Brian Mathew, Michael Joseph 1982
Lilies, Their Care & Cultivation, Michael Jefferson-Brown, Cassell 1990
Lilies of the World, H. D. Woodcock and W. T. Stearn, London 1950
Les Liliacées, Pierre-Joseph Redouté, Paris 1802-16
Lilies, A Revision of Elwes' Monograph, Patrick Synge, Batsford 1980
Lilies, A Kew Gardening Guide, Victoria Matthews,
Kew and Collingridge 1989
A Monograph of the Genus Lilium, Henry J. Elwes, London 1877-80
Lilies, Jan de Graaff and Edward Hyams, London 1967
The Lily Year Book of the North American Lily Society, 1948-present
The Lilies of Eastern Asia, Ernest Wilson, London 1925
Lilies for Every Garden, Isabella Preston, New York 1947
The Royal Horticultural Society's Lily Year Book, 1932-present
The Lilies of China, Stephen G. Haw, Batsford 1986
The International Lily Register, Royal Horticultural Society, 1982

Acknowledgments

The producers gratefully acknowledge the following individuals,
organizations, and sources that have assisted in the
creation of this book.

For the supply of photographs :
Brian Mathew.
The International Bloembollen Center,
Hillegom, The Netherlands.
Harry Smith, Horticultural Photographic Collection,
Hyde Hall, Rettenden, Essex, U.K.
Phillip Cribb.
Edward McCrae, Van der Salm Bulb Farm,
Woodland, Washington, U.S.A.
Derek Fox, Bullwood Nursery, Hockley, Essex, U.K.

For the creation of original illustrations:
Julia Cobbold

For the coloring & enhancement of archive illustrations:
Robin Harris

For pictorial references & visual material:
The Natural History of Plants, Kerner & Oliver,
The Gresham Publishing Co. 1904
The Gardener's Assistant, William Watson,
The Gresham Publishing Co. 1908
The Dover Pictorial Archive Series
Blumen Brueghel, Fritz Baumgart, DuMont Buchverlag Köln. 1978
Botanical Illustration, Ronald King, Ash & Grant. 1978
The Complete Encyclopaedia of Illustration,
J. G. Heck, Merehurst Press. 1988